You are in a place where the temperature is more than 38° Celsius. Sweat trickles down your face. You can even feel the heat through the soles of your boots. In the distance, you see what look like wavy, blurry lines rising from a dry, salt-covered lake bed. Everything looks tan or light brown. You see sand dunes, volcanic craters, prickly cactuses, and wild burros. You also see rocks. The valley floor is made of rocks, and so are the mountains around the valley. You are in one of the hottest and driest of all the American deserts.

Ubehebe Crater

Devil's Golf Course

Death Valley

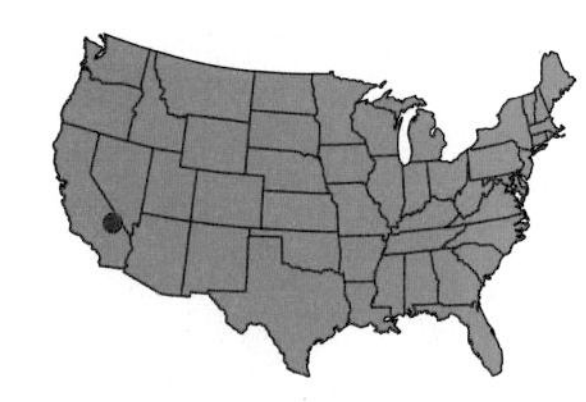

The earliest inhabitants of Death Valley were American Indians. Some of them called this place Tomesha, which means "ground afire." They learned how to live in the sparse, hot, dry desert. But some pioneers on their way to the California gold fields in the 1800s were unfamiliar with the valley and found it a frightful place. According to one story, some families traveling by wagon train became lost in the valley. They feared for their lives in the punishing heat. When they found their way out, one woman said, "Goodbye, Death Valley." That is how it got its name.

Death Valley is the hottest and driest place in North America. It is a land of ever-changing color. It is also a special place to sit on a rock and wonder.

- What are rocks made of?
- How are rocks made?
- How do rocks change?

Skidoo Mill

Unit D

ROCKS & MINERALS

Activities

Features

Chapter 1

Minerals

Death Valley is a place with many kinds of rocks and minerals. A mineral is a solid material found in the earth's crust. In the 1800s, people came to Death Valley searching for a highly prized mineral—gold. They searched for gold in the rocks of the surrounding mountains. They even discovered gold in dry streambeds. People who found gold were very lucky because gold is rare and valuable.

Some people came to Death Valley looking for another mineral called borax. Borax is less valuable and more plentiful than gold.

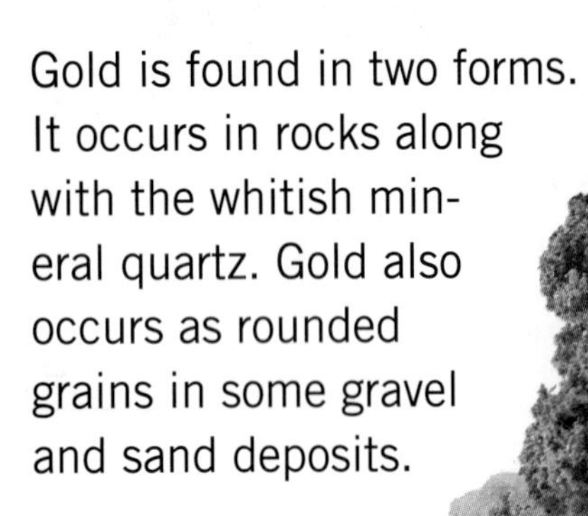

Gold is found in two forms. It occurs in rocks along with the whitish mineral quartz. Gold also occurs as rounded grains in some gravel and sand deposits.

Ruins of the Keane Wonder Mill

Lost Burro Gold Mine

Borax is used to make soaps and cleansers. It is also used in making glass. During the 1800s, Death Valley supplied most of the borax used in the United States.

Rainwater and streams wash pieces of rocks and minerals down onto the floor of the valley from the surrounding mountains. Like borax, these rocks and minerals are called deposits. These pieces of rocks and minerals form gravel and sand deposits.

SCIENCE JOURNAL What is sand? In your Science Journal, describe a place where you have seen sand. What did the sand look like? How did it feel?

What minerals are found in sand?

Process Skills
Classifying, Estimating, Making a graph

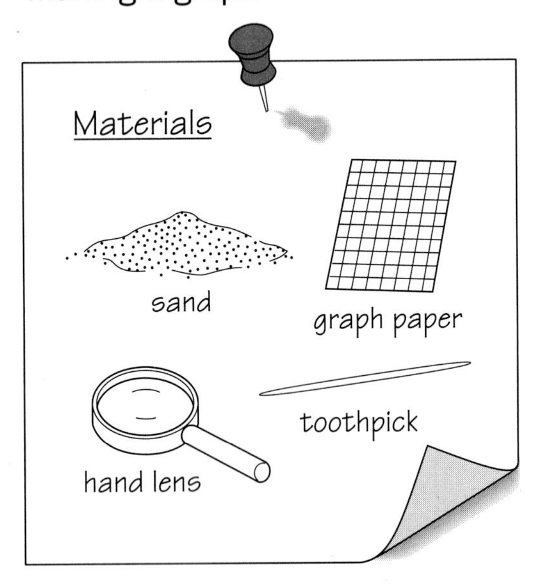

Observe and Collect Data

1. Obtain a sand sample. Spread it out on the graph paper.
2. Examine the particles of sand with a hand lens. Each particle is a sample of a particular mineral. Observe their different colors and shapes.
3. Use the table to help you identify the minerals found in the sand. Use a toothpick to sort the grains into piles of different minerals. Label each pile with the mineral name.
4. Use a toothpick to spread out one pile so that the grains are touching, but not on top of one another. Count the number of grains in one square of the graph paper. Use this information to estimate the total number of grains of that mineral. For example, if there are 20 grains in one square and the pile covers 4 squares, then there are $20 \times 4 = 80$ grains of that mineral. Record the mineral and the number of grains in a data table.
5. ACTIVITY JOURNAL Use the process in step 4 to determine the number of grains of each mineral. Record these data in your Activity Journal. Use your data to make a bar graph showing the mineral composition of your sand sample.

Share Your Results

How does your bar graph compare with those of your classmates?

Draw Conclusions

What is the most common mineral in your sand sample?

Apply What You Know

Do you think that all sand grains have the same minerals in them? Explain your answer.

Mineral	Most Common Color and Shape
biotite mica	brown to black; flat plates or sheets
muscovite mica	white, light gray, clear; flat plates or sheets
quartz	colorless, white; rounded or angular grains
calcite	white; rounded or angular grains
feldspar	white to gray to pink; rounded or angular grains

What are minerals?

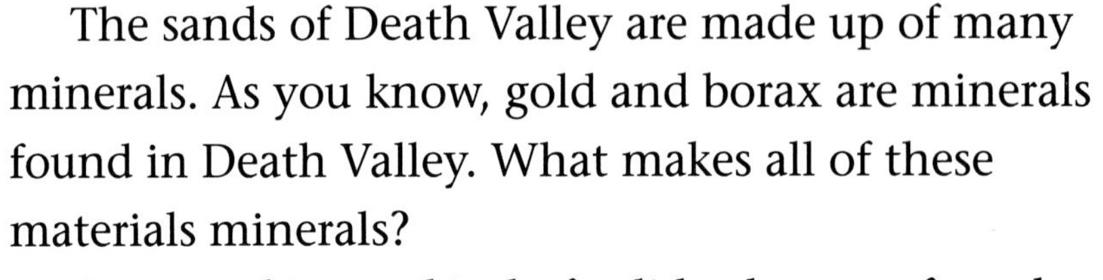

The sands of Death Valley are made up of many minerals. As you know, gold and borax are minerals found in Death Valley. What makes all of these materials minerals?

A mineral is one kind of solid substance found in the earth. To be a mineral, a substance must be nonliving and must occur in nature. It also must be made up of a set amount of ingredients, or parts, called elements. An element is the simplest of substances found on the earth. It cannot be broken down into a simpler substance.

Some minerals are made of a single element. Gold, for example, is a mineral that is a single element. Most minerals are formed from two or more elements that are joined together. Quartz, a mineral found in sand, is made up of the elements silicon and oxygen.

The earth's rocks are made up of minerals. They contain several thousand different minerals. However, some minerals are more common than others.

◀ If you have looked at table salt through a hand lens, you know that it is made up of tiny box-shaped pieces. Most minerals are made up of such solid shapes, called **crystals.** Different minerals are made up of different crystal shapes.

Halite

Garnet

Calcite

Feldspar

Quartz

Hornblende

▲ These pictures show some crystal shapes that are found in minerals. Minerals have different shapes because the tiny particles of the elements that make up each mineral are arranged in set patterns.

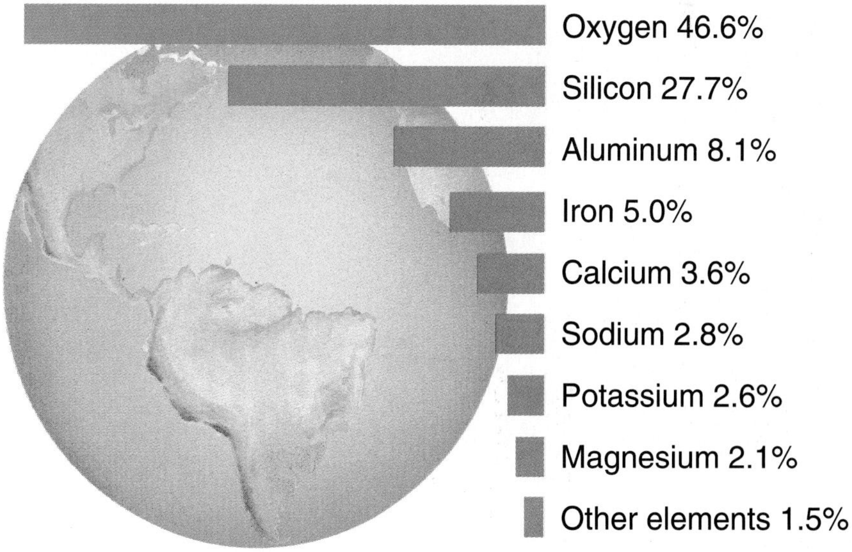

► This chart shows the most common elements in the earth's rocks. Which two elements are found in the greatest amount? Minerals that contain silicon and oxygen, such as feldspar, are very common.

Oxygen 46.6%
Silicon 27.7%
Aluminum 8.1%
Iron 5.0%
Calcium 3.6%
Sodium 2.8%
Potassium 2.6%
Magnesium 2.1%
Other elements 1.5%

How do minerals form?

The Devil's Golf Course is an ancient lake bed that is more than 160 kilometers long.

Did you know that you can "hear" the minerals in some parts of Death Valley? At the base of the Black Mountains, the floor of the valley looks and sounds very strange. This spot is called the Devil's Golf Course. It isn't a place to play golf—it is a place where minerals grow. How do you think minerals grow?

Although they are not living things, minerals form by growing. They do not grow in the same way that plants and animals do. They grow, or crystallize, from a liquid made up of water and one or more elements. This liquid can form as water flows over rocks and dissolves the minerals in the rocks. The minerals are carried away in the water as elements. When the water evaporates, the elements can form minerals again, which grow as crystals.

Now it is easier to understand why crystals grow at the Devil's Golf Course. In prehistoric times, it was a lake rich in the elements sodium and chlorine. When the lake dried up, a crust of salt crystals more than 1 meter thick formed. On warm days, you can hear a crackling noise made by the drying and expanding salt crust!

Be a Scientist

Can you make crystals?

1. 

Observe some table salt with a hand lens. Record your observations in your Activity Journal.
2. Fill a jar with hot tap water. Stir in one spoonful of table salt. Then continue to add salt until no more dissolves.
3. Tie a nail to a piece of string. Tie the other end of the string to the middle of a pencil. Place the pencil across the top of the jar so that the nail hangs into the water. The nail should not be touching the bottom of the jar.
4. Place the jar in a warm place, such as on a sunny window ledge. After a few days, describe in your Activity Journal what you see on the string.

Forces in the earth can cause rocks to heat up and melt. When the melted rock material cools, new minerals crystallize. The longer the material takes to cool, the larger the crystals grow. These crystals of the mineral olivine grew as melted rock cooled. ▼

Olivine

How are you doing?

1. Name two things that must be true for a substance to be a mineral.
2. How is gold different from quartz?
3. **Think** If one quartz crystal is twice as large as another one, what can you say about the ways each formed?

What are the properties of minerals?

White quartz

Rose quartz

Amethyst

◀ The differences in color in these three quartz samples are due to impurities in the minerals.

Gold and pyrite

How did the gold seekers in Death Valley recognize gold when they found it? Color was one way. But look at the pictures of gold and pyrite. Pyrite, a mineral made up of iron and sulfur, is called fool's gold. It fooled many gold seekers. Why do you think they were fooled?

Minerals are identified by properties. Color is one property. However, two different minerals, such as gold and pyrite, may have the same color. Also, impurities, or other elements not normally found in a mineral, can change that mineral's color. Observe the pictures of the three pieces of quartz. Using only the property of color, you might think that these were different minerals.

Some of the other properties used to identify minerals are shown here. These properties include the shapes of the crystals and how shiny the minerals are. Scientists look at several properties of a mineral to identify it.

Bornite

Talc

Gypsum

When some minerals are rubbed on a piece of unglazed tile, they leave a colored line. The color of this line is called **streak.** A mineral's streak does not change, even when impurities appear in the mineral. Compare the streaks produced by hematite on the left and pyrite on the right. Why is streak a useful property for identifying minerals? ▼

▲ Some minerals reflect light the way shiny metal does. Other minerals appear glassy or dull. The way a mineral reflects light is called **luster.** How would you describe the luster of gypsum, talc, and bornite?

SCIENCE JOURNAL

Choose five objects in your home. What word would you use to describe the luster of each? In your Science Journal, make a table that includes the name of each object and a description of its luster. Use descriptions such as shiny, metallic, glassy, dull, pearly, and silky.

BACK HOME

What are other properties of minerals?

If you compared a piece of gold with a piece of talc of the same size, you could feel that the gold is heavier than the talc. The **density** of a mineral is how heavy it is compared with how much space it takes up. You can use density to compare two minerals of the same size by lifting them. The mineral that seems heavier is denser. Scientists often measure density to help them identify minerals.

Many other properties can be used to help identify minerals. They include taste, smell, and whether the mineral is attracted to a magnet. What mineral do you think has a salty taste? **Hardness** is another property used to help identify minerals. When two minerals are rubbed together, the harder mineral will scratch the softer mineral.

Be a Scientist

Can you find mineral hardness?

Your teacher will give you some mineral samples. Scratch the samples against each other to see which one is hardest. Try to scratch each mineral with your fingernail and with a penny. In your Activity Journal, list the minerals in order, from hardest to softest. Indicate which minerals could be scratched by a fingernail and which could be scratched by a penny.

Mica

Galena

◀ Some minerals tend to break along flat surfaces. This property is called **cleavage.** Mica splits into thin sheets. It has cleavage in one direction, along the flat surface. Galena has cleavage in three directions. It breaks into small box-shaped pieces.

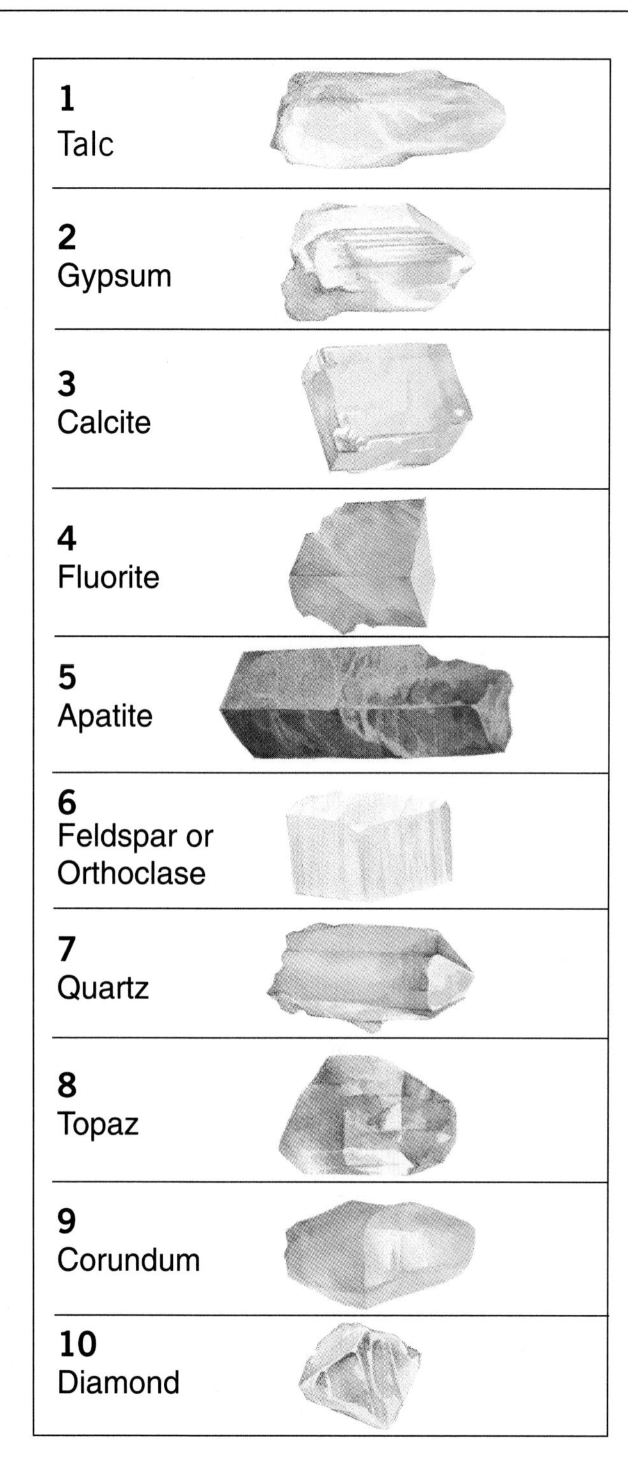

A fingernail has a hardness of 2.5 and will scratch softer minerals. A penny has a hardness of 3; a nail file, 5.5; and glass, less than 6.

Obsidian

Tremolite

▲ Most minerals tend to break along curved or uneven surfaces rather than flat ones. This property is called **fracture.** Obsidian (əb sid′ē ən) fractures along curved surfaces, as glass does. Some minerals, like tremolite, break the way wood does, into splinters or thin pieces.

◀ Scientists use a hardness scale, called the **Mohs'** (mōz) **scale**, to rate a mineral's hardness. The softest mineral on the scale is talc. It has a hardness of 1. Diamond, with a hardness of 10, is the hardest mineral on the scale. You can rate the hardness of any mineral by finding out which minerals it will scratch and which it will not scratch.

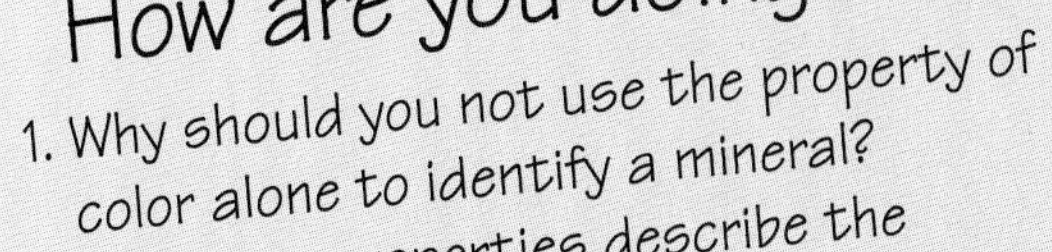

How are you doing?

1. Why should you not use the property of color alone to identify a mineral?
2. What two properties describe the way minerals break?
3. **Think** If a mineral sample scratches apatite, but does not scratch corundum, what can you say about its hardness?

How are minerals used?

Look around your classroom. Do you see any metal furniture? Is there glass in the windows? Are some classmates wearing jewelry? If you answered yes to any of these questions, there are probably minerals all around you. Minerals have many uses. Some uses are shown here.

Minerals are used in making powders and paints. ▶

▲ The mineral gypsum is used to make plaster, a chalky product used in construction.

▲ For hundreds of years, precious metals, such as gold and silver, have been used to make coins and jewelry. Copper and platinum are also precious metals.

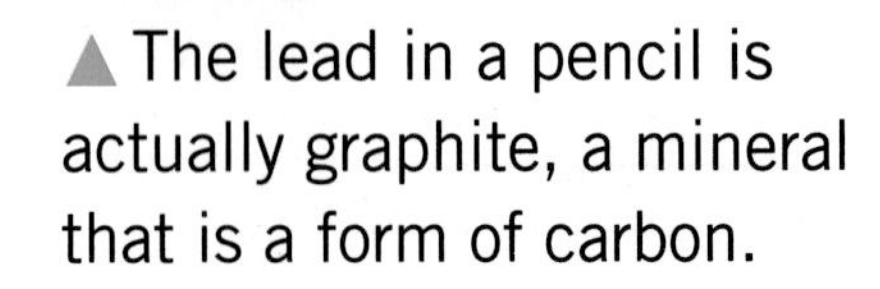

▲ The lead in a pencil is actually graphite, a mineral that is a form of carbon.

Bauxite is a mineral that contains aluminum, which is used to make cans, automobile parts, and building materials. ▶

Some minerals, called gemstones, are valued because they are hard, colorful, or rare. Diamonds, sapphires, rubies, and emeralds are gemstones. They are often cut, polished, and used to make jewelry.

▲ Did you know that you have quartz to thank for the windows you look out each day? Quartz, taken mostly from sand, is melted and used in making glass. Stained glass contains pigments from rocks. The lead between the pieces of glass is from a mineral called galena.

Turquoise is used to make stone carvings and jewelry. ▶

▲ Iron is used to make many products, including railways and nails. Some nails are coated with zinc so they won't rust.

Corundum is a very hard mineral that is used to make sandpaper.

What are ores?

Ores are minerals from which metals can be removed. Borax is an ore that was once obtained from Death Valley. Removing an ore from the earth is called mining. After the ores are mined, the needed metals are removed. Ores can be crushed, then melted and mixed to produce metals.

HISTORY

SCIENCE TECHNOLOGY & SOCIETY

Early People Used Pigments

People of ancient cultures crushed rocks to obtain pigments, or colored minerals. Makeup containing pigments has been used for thousands of years. Ancient Egyptians used eye makeup called kohl. Kohl was made from galena, which contains lead, and from charcoal. A green mineral called malachite was applied under the eyes. Malachite contains copper. During the Middle Ages, some artists used ground pyrite to make paint that looked like gold.

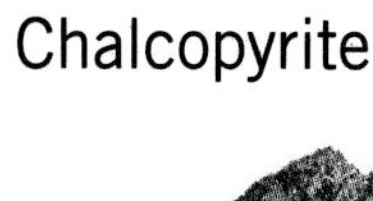

Chalcopyrite

Cassiterite

Bronze

Thousands of years ago, people learned that mixing copper and tin produced a harder metal. That metal, called bronze, is still used today. Do you have a brass lamp or brass doorknobs in your home? Brass is made by mixing copper and zinc.

Have you ever had your temperature taken when you were ill? The thermometer may have contained the element mercury. Another instrument, a barometer, contains mercury and it measures air pressure. Mercury comes from a red ore called cinnabar. Once removed from this ore, mercury is processed and becomes a silver-colored liquid.

▲ Copper, a metal, comes from seven kinds of mineral ores, including chalcopyrite and bornite. Once removed from the ores, copper is used to make many things, including wire and water pipes. If copper is melted and mixed with another metal, it is called an alloy. Copper and tin (cassiterite) mixed together make bronze, an alloy.

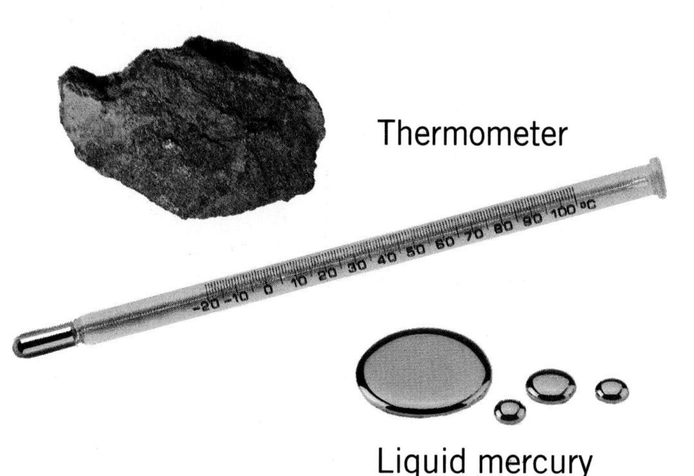

Cinnabar ore

Thermometer

Liquid mercury

How are you doing?

1. What are three precious metals?
2. From what mineral is mercury obtained?
3. **Think** If you were a sculptor and wanted to make a bronze statue, what metals would you use? Or if you wanted to make a brass part for a boat, what metals would you need?

Science & Literature Connection

Talking Walls

by Margy Burns Knight

This book shows many different ways in which people around the world use stone walls.

When this Aborigine boy was eight years old, he placed his hand next to his father's handprint and spread apart his small brown fingers. Then he blew a chalky white powder between his fingers onto the wall. He is very proud to return and find his handprint on the rock wall.

This rock wall and many others like it in Australia are covered with handprints and a collection of figures: skeletal fish, darting kangaroos, and people on horseback. Aborigines, descendants of Australia's first people, read their history in these paintings, some of which are more than thirty thousand years old.

Many paintings tell stories of the Aborigines' love of the land and of how they and their ancestors have always taken good care of the earth. Other, more recent paintings, tell of a terrible time when settlers came by ship with guns and took the land away from them. Today Aborigines continue to tell their stories with wall and tree-bark paintings.

Think About Your Reading

1. Why do you think Aborigines painted their history on rocks, rather than on cloth or paper? Why might an Aborigine boy be proud to put his handprint on a rock wall?
2. What does the book title, *Talking Walls*, mean to you?

Observing and communicating

What kind of handprint do you think your hand would make? Do you see any pattern in the lines of your palm and fingers? Write a description of what your handprint might look like.

Where to Read More

Alice Walker, *Finding the Green Stone* (Harcourt Brace Jovanovich, 1991) Johnny has lost his special stone, and that means trouble!

Looking Back

Words and Concepts

Fill in the blank with the word that best completes the sentence.

1. A(n) _______ is a nonliving, solid material made of elements found in the earth's crust.
2. The most common elements found in minerals are _______ and oxygen.
3. Halite is made of tiny box-shaped _______.
4. Minerals _______ out of a liquid made of water and one or more elements.
5. The property that describes how light is reflected from a mineral is called _______.
6. _______ are minerals from which metals are removed.

Applied Thinking Skills

Answer the following questions. You can use words, drawings, and diagrams in your answers.

7. Rubies and sapphires are both examples of the mineral corundum. Why are these minerals different colors?
8. What properties could you use to identify a mineral without looking at it?
9. Why might you expect quartz and glass to have similar hardness ratings on the Mohs' scale?
10. **Your World** Minerals are also found in food. They help keep your body healthy and strong. How would you find out what minerals are in broccoli, rice, and raisins?

Show What You Know

How can minerals be identified?

Observe and Collect Data

1. Obtain five numbered mineral samples. Your job is to identify properties of these minerals and then identify the minerals.
2. In your Activity Journal, describe the color of each mineral. Then describe its luster. You might use the words *metallike, glassy,* and *dull.* Then use the streak plate to test each mineral.
3. Estimate the hardness of each mineral. Use a penny, your fingernail, the quartz sample, and the scale on page D17 to do this.
4. Describe cleavage, fracture, or any crystal shape that you observe for each mineral.
5. Use references to identify your minerals.

Process Skills

Observing, Classifying, Inferring

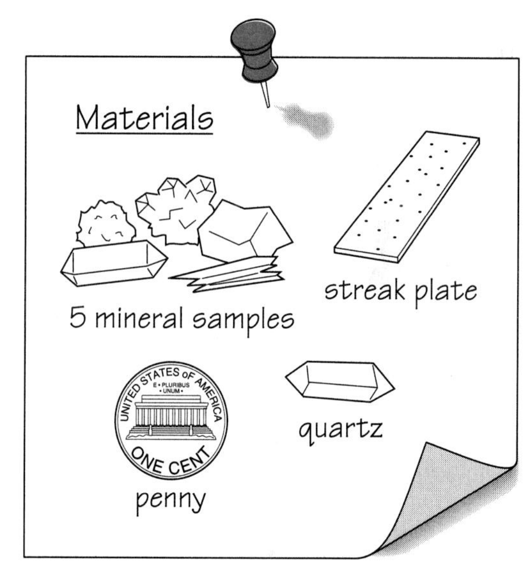

Draw Conclusions

1. Compare your samples and descriptions with those of your classmates. How are your descriptions for the same minerals similar or different?
2. How useful were the properties in helping you identify the minerals?

The desert's rocky floor

Rocks in upper Warm Springs Canyon are made of granite.

Chapter 2

Rocks

Have you ever heard of a rockhound? A rockhound is a person who collects rocks. Each year, many of these curious rock hunters come to Death Valley to study rocks. This is not surprising—everywhere you look in Death Valley, you see rocks. You even get rocks in your shoes as you hike along the desert trails.

Rocks are solid materials that are made up of one or more minerals. Although some rocks are made up of a single mineral, most rocks are mixtures of minerals. Granite is one type of rock found in Death Valley. Notice that granite is made up of many different-colored crystals, which are different kinds of minerals. Quartz, feldspar, and mica are all minerals that make up granite.

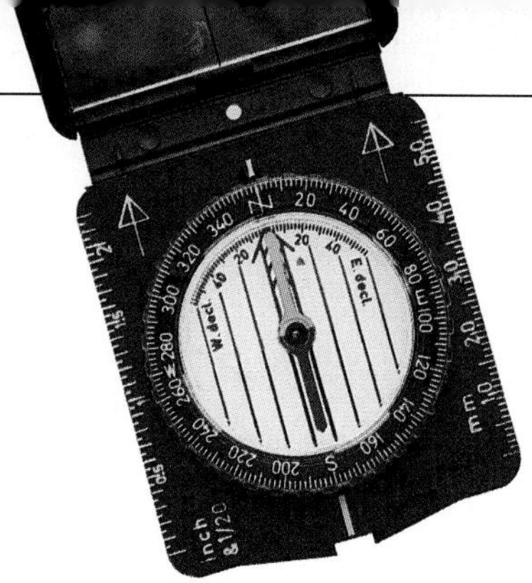

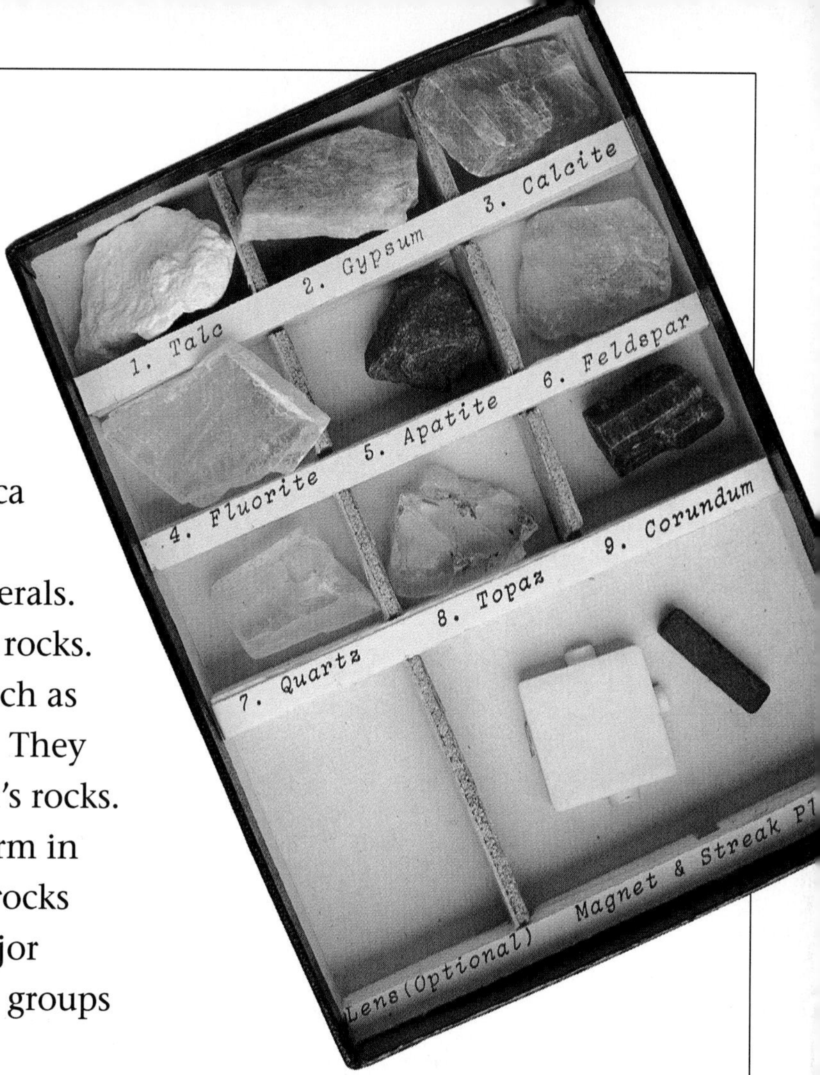

There are more than 2,000 kinds of minerals. Yet only a few of them make up the earth's rocks. Minerals containing oxygen and silicon, such as feldspar and quartz, are the most common. They are found in more than half of all the earth's rocks. There are many kinds of rocks, and they form in many different ways. Scientists who study rocks usually classify, or sort, rocks into three major groups. Rocks are classified into these three groups by the way they formed.

SCIENCE JOURNAL

Do you collect anything? Do you know someone who collects stamps, baseball cards, dolls, or other objects? If you have a collection, describe in your Science Journal how you sort the things in it. If you would like to have a collection, describe how you would organize it.

1. Talc
2. Gypsum
3. Calcite
4. Fluorite
5. Apatite
6. Feldspar
7. Quartz
8. Topaz
9. Corundum
Lens (Optional)
Magnet & Streak Pl

Mica

Feldspar

Quartz

Explore Activity

HANDS-ON ACTIVITY

How can you classify rocks?

Process Skills
Observing, Classifying, Communicating

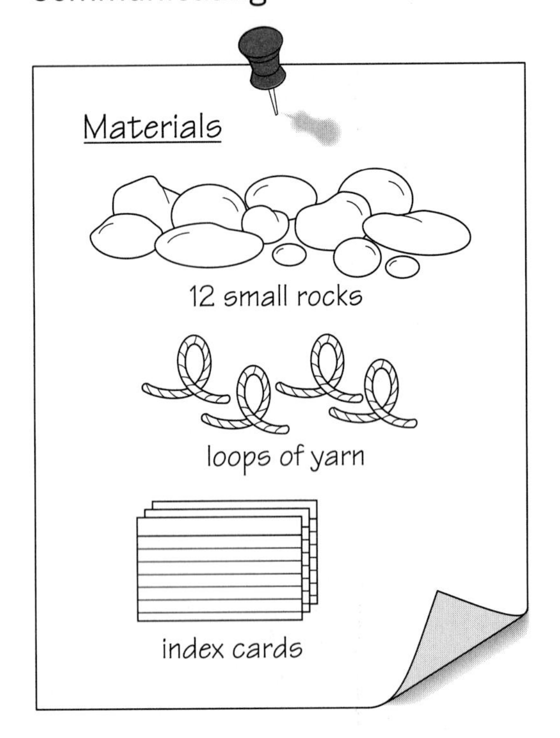

Observe and Collect Data

1. Spread the rocks out on a table. Examine them. Think of a property you could use to sort, or classify, the rocks. For example, you could sort the rocks by color.
2. Place several loops of yarn on the table so that they form circles. Based on your property sort the rocks and then group them inside the loops.
3. Make an index card that describes the property for each group of rocks. Place each card at the top of the loop of rocks that it describes.
4. ACTIVITY JOURNAL In your Activity Journal, make a drawing that shows your results. Your drawing should include the index cards and the number of rocks in each loop.
5. Turn the index cards over. Have the members of another group examine the rocks in your loops. Have them name the property you used to sort. Turn over the index cards so that others can see if they named the correct property.

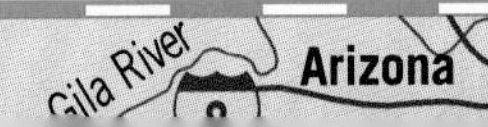

Share Your Results

Were other groups able to name your group's property? What might this say about the property you chose or how well you sorted your rocks?

Draw Conclusions

1. What properties did the other groups in your class use to sort their rocks?
2. If you used another group's property to sort your rocks, would the same rocks sort within the same loops? Explain.

Apply What You Know

Why do you think it is important that all scientists use the same set of properties to classify rocks?

How do igneous rocks form?

Can you imagine hiking inside the crater of a volcano? You can do this at Death Valley. Inside Ubehebe Crater, rocks of every size lie in jumbles and piles. The crater formed when molten rock mixed with ground water and the superheated water changed to steam and blew out rocks, cinders, and ash.

Beneath the earth's surface is melted rock. This melted rock is called magma (mag´mə). At times, magma reaches the earth's surface through cracks in the earth's surface or through volcanoes. As pressure builds up inside the earth, magma can be forced upward through a channel, or vent, in the volcano. When magma leaves the volcano, it is called lava. Lava may explode outward from the volcano. Or it may flow down the sides of the volcano. As lava cools, it hardens and forms rock.

Magma also can slowly cool and harden under the earth's surface. When this happens, it also forms rock.

Rock that forms when magma or lava cools and hardens is called **igneous** (ig´nē əs) **rock.** Most of the rock in the earth's outer layer is igneous. Most of this rock is just below the earth's surface.

These two pictures show Ubehebe Crater. It is shaped like a basket. It is about 530 meters wide at the rim and 240 meters deep. Note how the sides of the crater have weathered. ▼

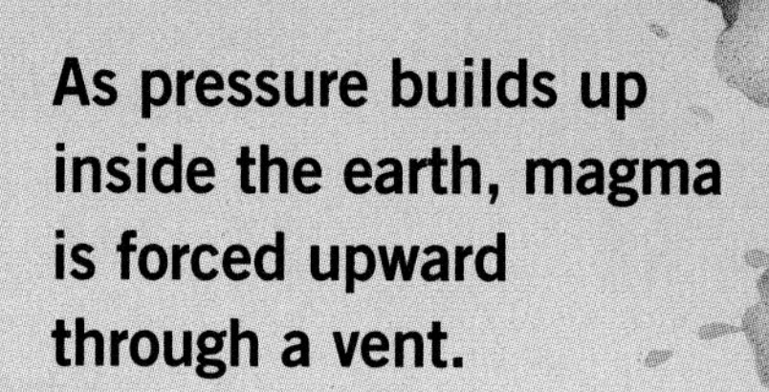

As pressure builds up inside the earth, magma is forced upward through a vent.

Lava may flow down the sides of the volcano or explode violently outward from the inside.

Lava, because it is on the earth's surface, tends to cool and harden more quickly. This kind of igneous rock formed from lava has very small crystals, often too small to see with your eyes alone.

Within the earth, magma generally cools and hardens slowly. As a result, it forms rocks with large crystals.

Lava flow

Vent

Rock layers

Ash layers

Earth layers

A pool of magma is found in the earth below the volcano.

What are some kinds of igneous rocks?

Many kinds of igneous rock are found on the earth's surface. The pictures on these pages show some of the most common kinds of igneous rocks. Igneous rocks are found as natural structures and in structures made by people.

Mt. Rushmore in South Dakota is carved from igneous rock.

Kilauea Volcano

To see an active volcano, you must leave Death Valley. Kilauea (kē´lou ā´ə) is an active volcano on the island of Hawaii. Lava from Kilauea flows quickly and spreads out before reaching the nearby ocean. As the lava from the volcano hardens, the igneous rock called basalt forms. It often hardens into a shape that looks like a smooth mass of ropes. All the Hawaiian Islands are islands formed by volcanoes.

Granite forms from magma that cools deep inside the earth. It has visible grains of minerals and varies in color from gray to red. Granite is used as a common building material.

Obsidian has a glassy surface and sharp edges. It was used by American Indians for arrow points, mirrors, and ornaments.

Basalt (bə sôlt´) forms from hardened lava. It is the most common volcanic rock on the earth. Many islands, like the Hawaiian Islands, are made of basalt.

All the tiny holes in pumice make it so light it floats in water!

Pumice (pum´is) forms when lava explodes from a volcano. It has many small holes left by trapped gases. Pumice is sometimes used in polishing materials.

How are you doing?

1. What are rocks made of?
2. What are two examples of igneous rocks?
3. **Think** You are given an igneous rock sample made up of large black and white crystals. What can you conclude about the way the rock formed?

How do sedimentary rocks form?

A kind of rock made of pieces of other rocks can be found at Zabriskie Point. Water and wind can wear away rock into tiny pieces. These pieces of rocks are called **sediments** (sed´ə məntz). Over time, wind and water can carry sediments far from the original rock.

A large lake once covered much of Death Valley. Sediments carried by wind, streams, and rain fell into the lake and sank to the bottom. The weight of the water and air above the sediments pressed the sediments together. This is called **compaction** (kəm pak´shən). Slowly, the layers of sediments were cemented together and became rock. This is known as **cementation** (sē´men tā´shən). Rocks that form from sediments or pieces of older rocks are called **sedimentary** (sed´ə men´tər ē) **rocks.**

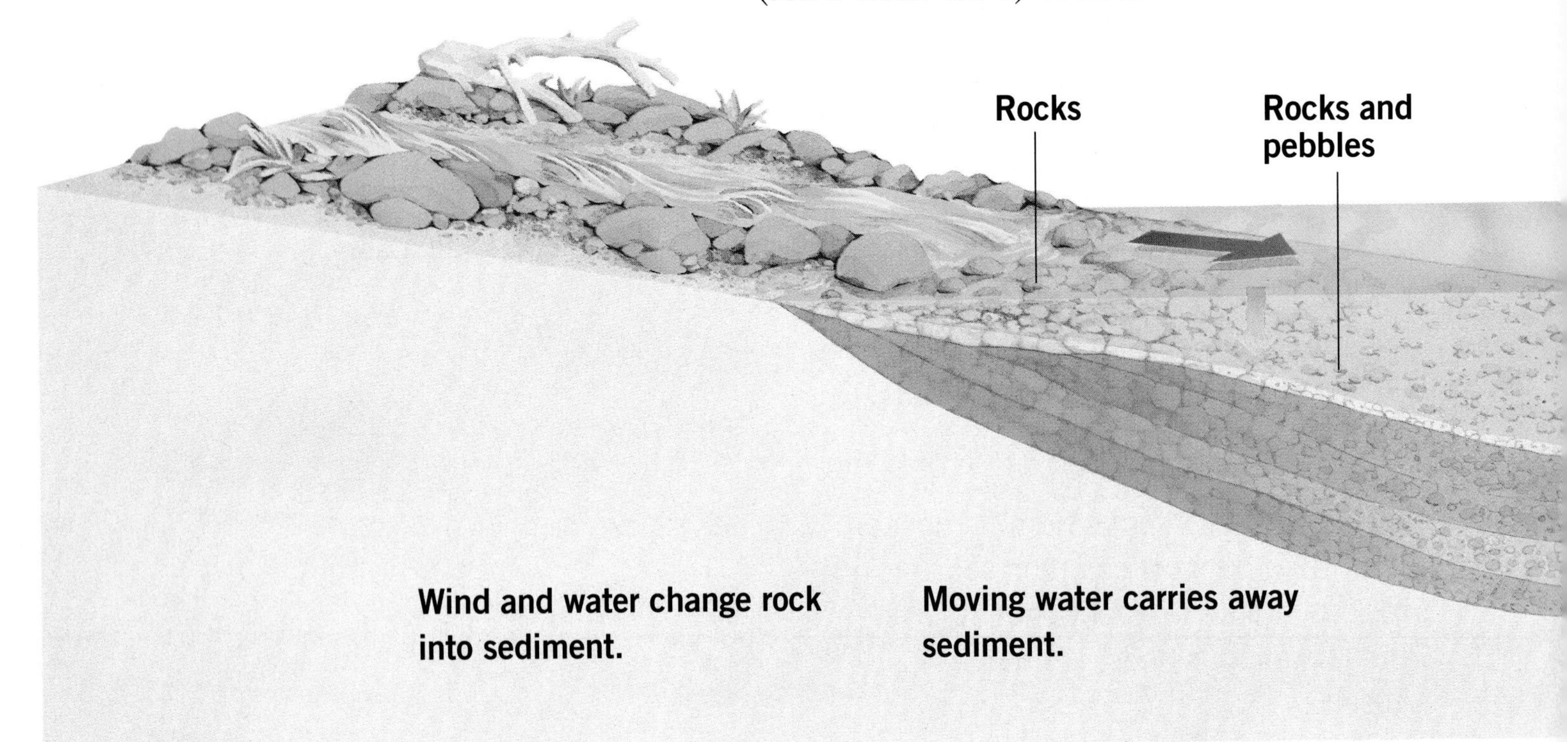

What cements sediments together? Sometimes compaction is enough to hold sediments together. At other times, when water flows over rocks, it dissolves minerals and carries away their elements. As the sediments become compacted, the water in the sediments evaporates and the minerals crystallize from dissolved elements, gluing sediment particles together. This process makes loose sediments into cemented rock.

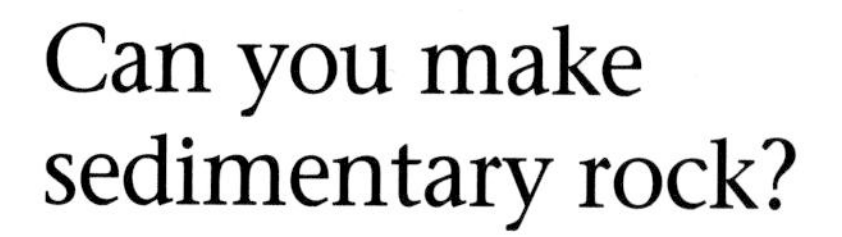

Be a Scientist

HANDS-ON ACTIVITY

Can you make sedimentary rock?

1. Place water, soil, sand, and gravel into a container that has a lid.
2. Put the lid on tightly and shake the container. Observe the container for 15 minutes. Leave the container in place overnight and observe it the next day.
3. ACTIVITY JOURNAL In your Activity Journal, make a drawing of what you see. How does your model show how sediment forms?

Sands

Silts

Muds

Dead plants and animals

Sediment settles to the bottom of a lake or sea.

Pressure and cementation change lower layers of sediment into rock.

What are some kinds of sedimentary rock?

Sandstone forms from grains of sand. It is used to make pottery, building materials, concrete, and road materials.

You have learned that sedimentary rocks form from sediments and dissolved minerals. Sandstone and shale are examples of such rocks. Sometimes dissolved minerals crystallize without sediments being present. The salt crust at the Devil's Golf Course is an example of this kind of sedimentary rock. Here the rock is called rock salt, and it is made up of the mineral halite. Another example of this kind of sedimentary rock is limestone.

Another way sedimentary rocks form is from the remains of animals and plants. As in the case of sediment particles, these remains can become compacted and cemented. Some limestones form this way, and so does coal.

Limestone forms from the shells of sea animals. It is used in concrete and road materials.

Rock gypsum is made mostly of the mineral gypsum. It is used in a building material called plasterboard.

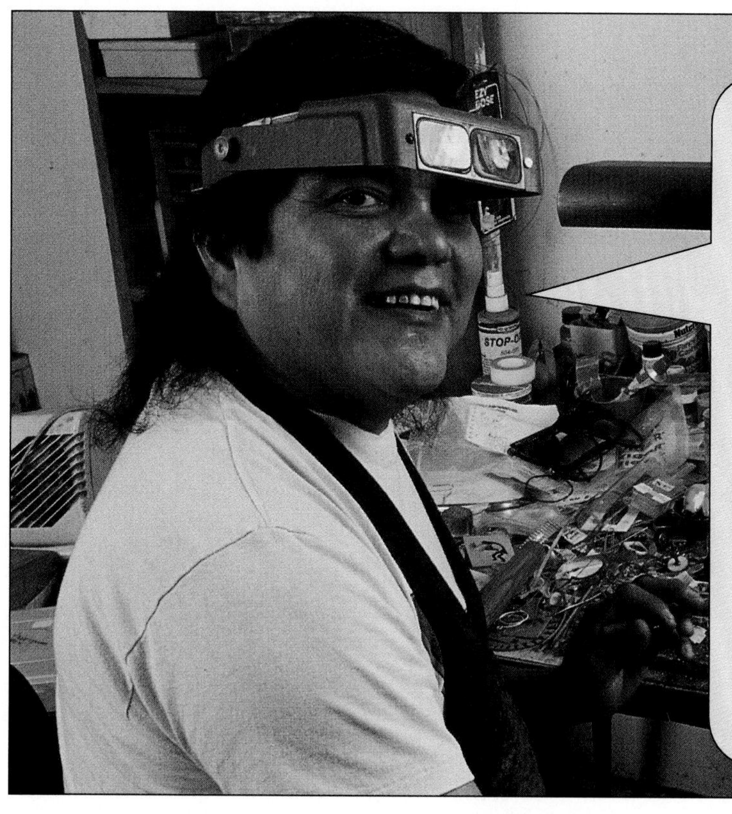

Career Corner

Silversmithing

My name is Joe Rosetta. I am a silversmith. I learned to work with minerals and gemstones when I was growing up in Santo Domingo Pueblo in New Mexico. I was taught to handle stones by my family. My father said it is good to learn this craft because it will always be with you. I enjoy creating pieces of art from silver, turquoise, and my imagination.

Where can you find sedimentary rocks? The answer to that question is easy. Just look around you! Sedimentary rocks cover about three quarters of the earth's land. Many buildings and everyday objects are made of sedimentary rocks. The pictures show some common kinds of sedimentary rocks and their uses.

Shale forms from mud. It is used in cement and bricks. Shale is often found with coal deposits.

How are you doing?

1. How do sediments form rocks?
2. What are two sedimentary rocks formed from some parts of plants and animals?
3. **Think** Some parts of sedimentary rocks come from recycling older rocks. How might you explain this?

How do metamorphic rocks form?

1. Rock becomes buried under the surface of the earth.

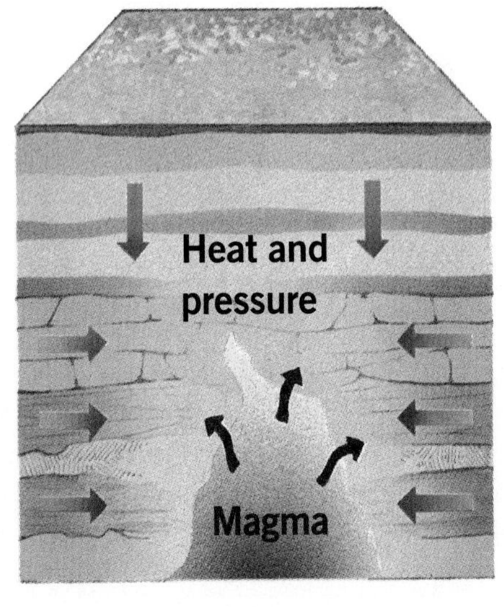

2. Great heat and pressure act on the rock deep within the earth.

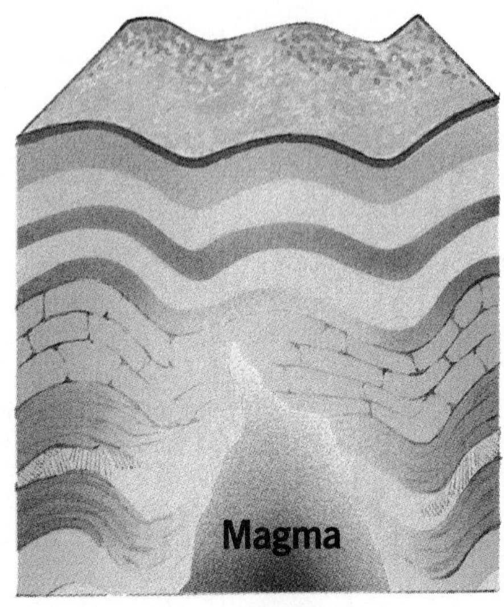

3. Rock slowly folds and changes into metamorphic rock.

Igneous and sedimentary rocks can form on the earth's surface. However, these same rocks later might be buried deep within the earth from natural events. When these rocks are buried, they begin to change. The weight of the rocks above presses down on rocks within the earth. Temperatures within the earth are very hot. Pressure and heat increase with depth in the earth's crust. Slowly, the pressure and heat change the rock into a new kind of rock. Rocks that form under pressure and heat within the earth are **metamorphic** (met´ə môr´fik) **rocks**.

Igneous and sedimentary rock can be changed, or transformed, into metamorphic rock. But did you know that metamorphic rock can be transformed into another kind of metamorphic rock? An older metamorphic rock can be transformed by heat and pressure into different kinds of metamorphic rock.

Looking east from Badwater in Death Valley, you can see a ridge of dark, craggy peaks called the Black Mountains. These

The steep sides of Titus Canyon are made of metamorphic rocks.

mountains are metamorphic rock. The rock formed far below the surface of the earth. Gradually, powerful forces within the earth pushed the mountains upward into the peaks you see today.

Be a Scientist

HANDS-ON ACTIVITY

Can you model a metamorphic rock?

1. Peel the paper off several pieces of different colored broken crayons and put the crayons into a small plastic bag.
2. Place the bag on top of several pebbles in a sunny spot or near a heater or lamp. Set a thin, flat rock on top of the bag. It should cover the crayons. The stone should get warm.
3. ACTIVITY JOURNAL Check the crayons after one day. In your Activity Journal, record your observations. A sketch might be helpful. You might want to make observations for two or three more days.

Is the house or building you live in made of rock? If it is, try to find out what kind of rock it is made of. If your home is not rock, find a nearby building that is. Try to figure out what kind of rock material was used to make the building. If possible, look at chimneys, foundations, and steps.

What are some kinds of metamorphic rocks?

Metamorphic rocks are found all over the world. People have used metamorphic rocks to make useful objects, such as tools and works of art. Ancient Greeks used marble for sculptures because it is easy to cut and polish. Some buildings,

Orange peels should not be thrown into the desert. They are not eaten by animals. They will dry, but will not disappear for years. Only leave footprints in the desert.

Slate is made of mica and quartz. It splits into thin sheets and is used for roofing material. Chalkboards were once made of slate.

Marble is made mainly of calcite and dolomite. It is often used for statues and building materials.

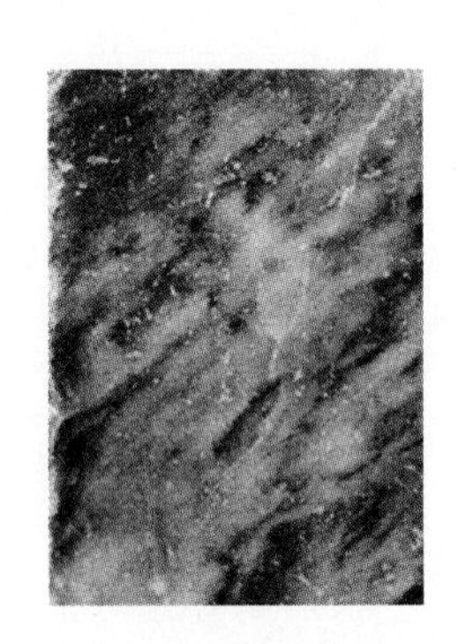

Soapstone is one of the softest rocks. This bear sculpture was carved from soapstone by 17-year-old Lance Yazzie, a Navaho.

Fragile Deserts

Deserts look tough. Yet they are fragile and show the effects of even one person's visit. You may be surprised by the many scars in the landscape near Death Valley. In the 1850s, gold, silver, and borax were mined in the desert. Since then, other rocks and minerals have been mined there. Mine holes were not filled, so the scars remain.

Think About It Death Valley is a national monument. It belongs to all people. Do you think that mining should be allowed in Death Valley? If mining is allowed, how do you think the scars from mining might be erased from the landscape? Write a letter stating your opinions to a newspaper.

Wildflowers covering a rocky slope

like the Taj Mahal in India, are made of marble. Rome also has many buildings made of marble.

How are you doing?

1. What kind of rock are metamorphic rocks made from?
2. What conditions change rocks into metamorphic rock?
3. **Think** Why does metamorphic rock that forms from sedimentary rock often have curving streaks of color in it?

A View from the Top

You climb to the top of Telescope Peak and you look far below you. You feel that you are on top of the world. You can see Ubehebe Crater, some sand dunes, Salt Creek, and Badwater. You know about the processes that formed the igneous, sedimentary, and metamorphic rocks in Death Valley. You know about minerals and their properties.

How might a geologist, a scientist who studies rocks and minerals, view Death Valley? What might interest a photographer? How would a historian see the valley? How would a park ranger look at Death Valley? If you were an American Indian living in Death Valley before the gold rush of the 1800s, how might you have viewed Death Valley? What might your point of view be today?

Data Collection and Analysis

How can you investigate a rock?

Rocks have many characteristics. How many can you describe? Get to know your own rock by discovering its volume, density, mass, and color.

Observe and Collect Data

1. 

Work with a group and list characteristics of your rock. Record this list in your Activity Journal.
2. Analyze your rock's characteristics. Have your procedures approved by your teacher before beginning the analysis.
3. Make a table in your Activity Journal. Add the results from three other groups to your table.

Draw Conclusions

1. What characteristics of your rock did you examine? Which ones were the hardest to describe and measure? Which ones were the easiest?
2. Which characteristic of your rock seems unique? Write a description of your rock so that someone who has never seen your rock can find it in a group of rocks.
3. Did you find that the rocks in your class were different or mostly the same? What might you have to do to get a wide range of differences among a group of rocks?

Looking Back

Words and Concepts

Fill in the blank with the word that best completes the sentence.

1. Solid materials made up of one or more minerals are called ____.
2. Rocks are classified by the way they ____ and the minerals in them.
3. Rock salt is a(n) ____ rock made up of halite.
4. As ____ cools on the earth's surface, it forms igneous rock.
5. Heat and ____ transform sedimentary rock into metamorphic rock.
6. ____ is a metamorphic rock made mostly of calcite and dolomite.

Applied Thinking Skills

Answer the following questions. You can use words, drawings, and diagrams in your answers.

7. Compaction does not play a part in the formation of which of the three kinds of rocks? Explain your answer.
8. What kind of rock would you expect to find on Surtsey, a volcanic island in Iceland?
9. Why don't metamorphic rocks form on the earth's surface?
10. **Your World** What rock forms from dissolved minerals?

Show What You Know

HANDS-ON ASSESSMENT

What is made from rocks and minerals?

Observe and Collect Data

1. Look through old magazines. Find a picture of an object that has many different parts.
2. Cut out the picture. Tape it to a sheet of paper.
3. Draw lines from five different parts of the object to open spaces on the paper.
4. At the end of each line, write the name of the material that part is made from. Then tell whether the material is from a rock or mineral, or from another material you can name.

Process Skills

Observing, Classifying, Inferring

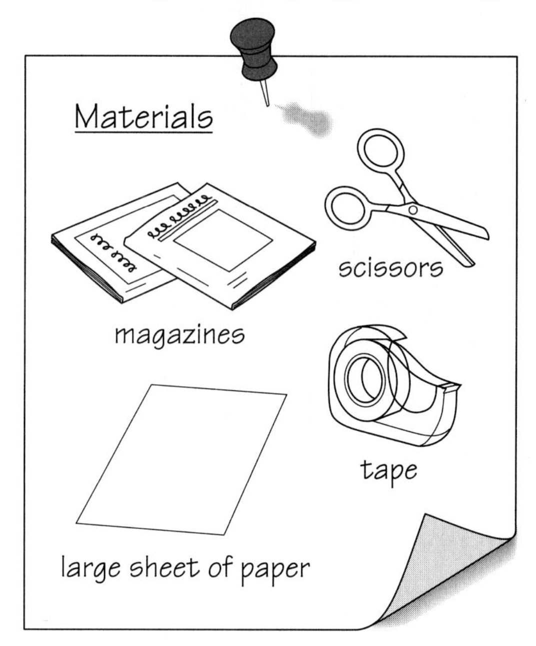

Draw Conclusions

1. What objects are made from rocks and minerals?
2. What do objects made from rocks and minerals have in common?

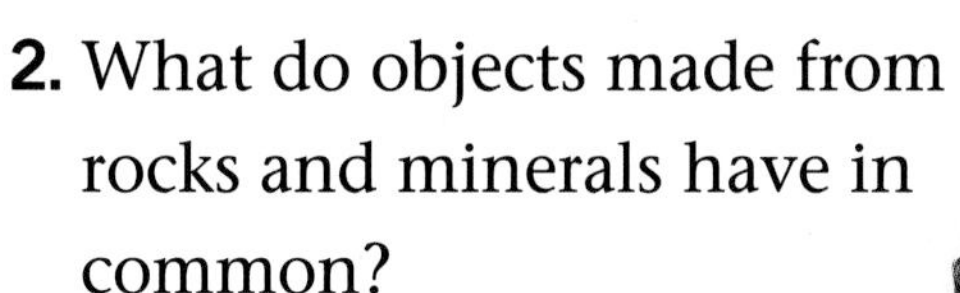

Chapter 3

The Rock Cycle

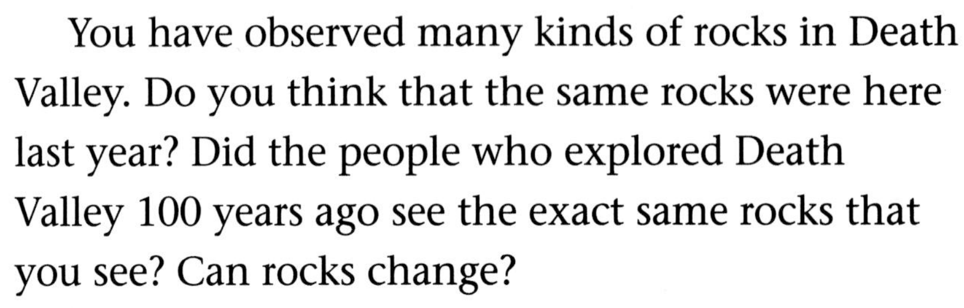

You have observed many kinds of rocks in Death Valley. Do you think that the same rocks were here last year? Did the people who explored Death Valley 100 years ago see the exact same rocks that you see? Can rocks change?

One example of how rocks change can be found near Desolation Canyon in Death Valley. This unusually shaped feature shown in the picture is called Mushroom Rock. It is made of basalt, which hardened from hot lava that flowed from an opening in the earth's surface. How do you think this rock got its mushroom shape?

Look at the picture of Mushroom Rock. In your Science Journal, describe how you think the rock might have changed. Why do you think such changes take place?

Mushroom Rock

Natural Bridge

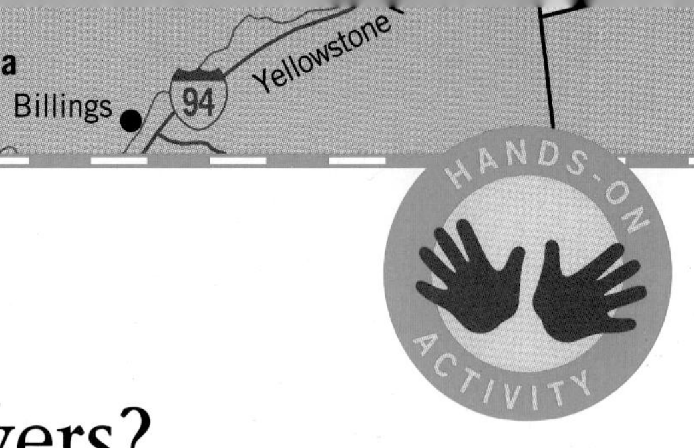

Explore Activity

How do rocks form layers?

Process Skills
Inferring, Controlling variables, Interpreting data

Observe and Collect Data

1. Put 2 spoonfuls of powdered clay into one cup, 2 spoonfuls of gravel into a second cup, 2 spoonfuls of salt into a third cup, and 2 spoonfuls of sand into a fourth cup.
2. Put 2 spoonfuls of each kind of material into the fifth cup.
3. Fill each cup with water and stir well.
4. ACTIVITY JOURNAL In your Activity Journal, make a table like the one shown. Record your observations in the table.

5. Record your observations again after 10, 20, and 30 minutes. Draw a diagram of the layers you see in the cup containing the mixture of materials.

Share Your Results

Do the mixtures of other groups look like yours? If not, how are they different?

Draw Conclusions

1. What happened in each container?
2. Which cup(s) model the carrying of dissolved minerals by water?
3. In what order do sand, clay, and gravel settle to the bottom of the glass?

Apply What You Know

What happens to clay, gravel, salt, and sand carried by streams?

Beginning	After 10 minutes	After 20 minutes	After 30 minutes
clay			
gravel			
salt			
sand			
mixture			

Mosaic Canyon

How do rocks change?

You have learned that rocks can change. Wind and water can wear away at rock, breaking it into tiny pieces. The wearing away of rock is called **weathering**. Wind, water, ice, and living things all help to weather rocks. When wind carrying bits of sand and other small pieces of rock material blows against rocks, the surface gets worn away.

◀ As rock particles in a stream bounce against each other, they become worn down and their edges become rounded.

What do you think happened to the rocks shown here? When pieces of rock are carried by water, they bounce off one another and off the bottom of the stream. As a result, the rocks are weathered. Observe the shapes of the small rocks in the picture. These rounded rocks are called gravel and are taken from a stream. How do you think they got their rounded shapes?

The wearing away of rock by the action of wind and moving water is called physical weathering. Ice also can cause physical weathering. Water expands, or gets larger, as it turns into ice. When water is trapped in cracks in rock, it presses and pushes on the rock as it freezes and expands. After a time,

▲ The cracks in this rock were caused by water that froze and expanded.

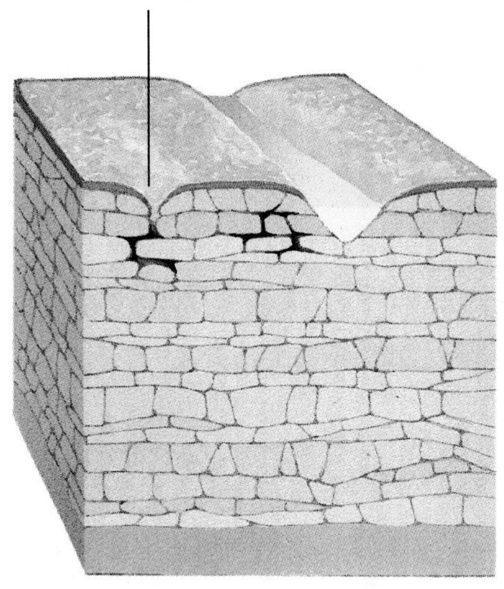

1. Water carrying acid sinks into limestone.

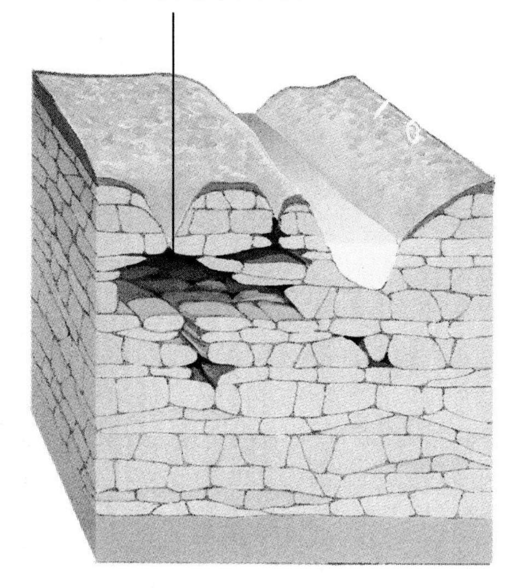

2. Minerals in the rock are dissolved and carried away.

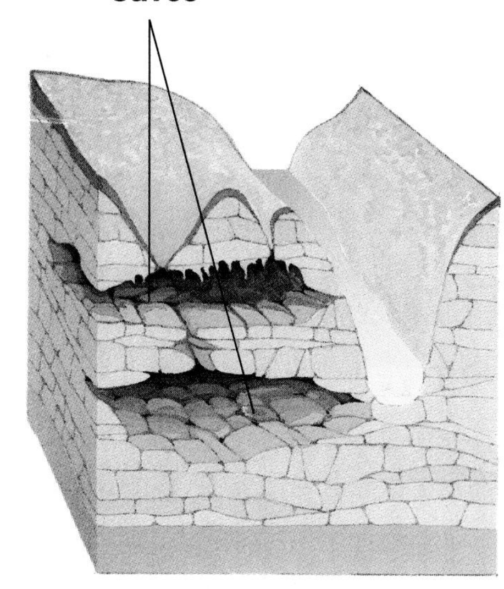

3. As minerals continue to dissolve, an underground cave forms.

the ice causes the cracks to grow larger, and the rock continues to crack and crumble.

Some kinds of weathering involve changes in the minerals that make up rocks. Weathering that results from changes in minerals is called chemical weathering. Rainwater can cause chemical weathering. Rainwater contains small amounts of a material called acid. Some kinds of rock, such as limestone, are eaten away by acid. This happens because minerals like calcite and dolomite dissolve easily in the acid. Observe in the drawings that rainwater sinking into the ground dissolves the underground limestone. Eventually, a cave forms.

Be a Scientist

HANDS-ON ACTIVITY

How does acid weather limestone?

1. Fill a cup about one-quarter full with vinegar.
2. Add a piece of chalk to the cup of vinegar.
3. 

In your Activity Journal, record your observations. A sketch might be helpful.

What else weathers rocks?

Smoke from factories and cars can join with rainwater to make acid. Rainwater that contains an extra amount of acid is called acid rain. Acid rain speeds chemical weathering.

Some plants grow on rocks. How do you think plants grow on rocks? Seeds fall into small cracks in the rocks. The seeds sprout and the growing plants and their roots push against the rocks. This pressure causes the cracks to get larger and sometimes break apart. So, as strange as it seems, growing plants can wear away rock material. The wearing down of rock by living things is called biological (bī´ə läj´i kəl) weathering. You probably have seen examples of this kind of weathering on sidewalks and steps.

The stone in this building is being cleaned of pollutants to stop chemical weathering.

Roots of plants can grow into cracks in rocks and cause pieces of rock to break off.

Tree roots can grow under sidewalks and cause the sidewalk to be uplifted or cracked.

SIDE TRIP

Mammoth Cave

There are limestone caves near Death Valley. But the largest limestone cave in the world is in Kentucky. The picture below shows just one room in Mammoth Cave, part of Mammoth Cave National Park. This underground cave system has more than 480 kilometers of explored and mapped passages. The limestone that makes up the cave formed about 240 million years ago. Water, including water from an underground river, began dissolving the limestone. For a time, the entire limestone cave was underwater. The waters finally lowered, leaving a cave and some underground lakes.

Weathering is a very slow process. You usually don't notice it happening. As the years pass, rocks are worn away. So rocks do not last forever. The weathering of rocks forms sediments, such as sand and gravel. As you might remember, sediments can join to form new rocks.

How are you doing?

1. What are the four ways that rocks weather?
2. What kind of weathering is caused by acid rain?
3. **Think** What will happen when water flows over halite? What do you think happens to the halite?

What is the rock cycle?

Igneous rock

Sedimentary rock

Metamorphic rock

It's true that most of the rocks on the earth's surface are sedimentary rocks. These rocks are worn away by weathering. The tiny sediments, or pieces, of rock that weathering creates get carried by wind or water and will come to rest on the earth's surface. As the weathered pieces build up and are pressed together, new sedimentary rock forms.

Sometimes sedimentary rock is forced deep into the earth. Heat and pressure deep below the surface can change sedimentary rock into metamorphic rock. What if the metamorphic rock got so hot that it melted and became magma? What kind of rock would form when the magma hardened?

Weathering can also wear away igneous rock and metamorphic rock found on the earth's surface. What kind of rock would form from the material that had been worn away?

Does it seem that any kind of rock can become any other kind of rock? It can. Under the right conditions, one type of rock can become another type of rock. The earth's rocks are always changing. Rocks are always being recycled. The process that causes one rock to become another rock is called the **rock cycle.** Look at the diagram on page D55 to see the ways that rocks can change.

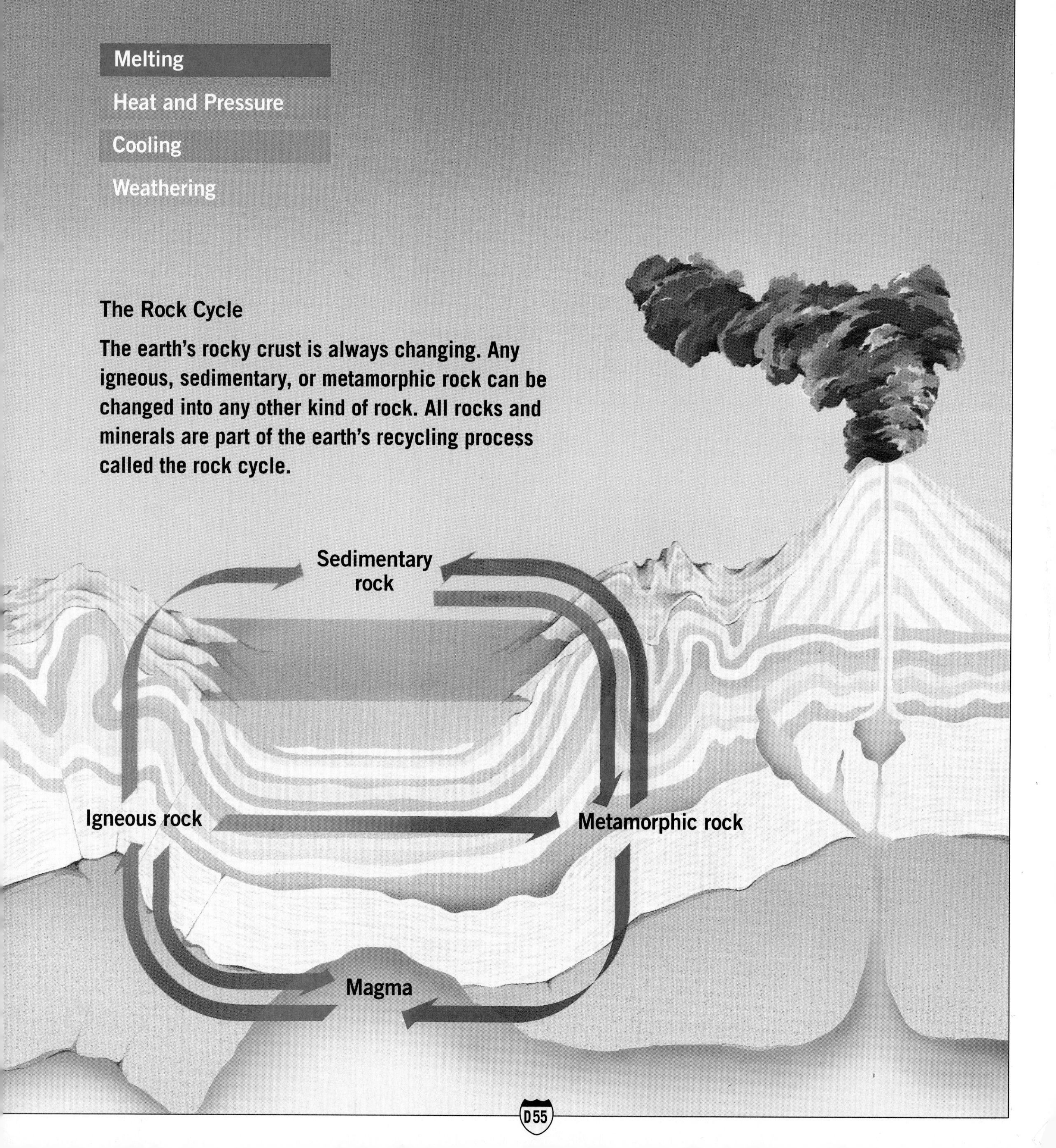

The Rock Cycle

The earth's rocky crust is always changing. Any igneous, sedimentary, or metamorphic rock can be changed into any other kind of rock. All rocks and minerals are part of the earth's recycling process called the rock cycle.

What happens to rocks in the rock cycle?

The drawings show how rocks might change during the rock cycle. As you read about each kind of change, turn to page D55 and follow the stages in the rock cycle diagram. For example, if granite is weathered, the pieces might form sandstone. This is a change from an igneous rock into a sediment by weathering, and a change from a sediment into a sedimentary rock.

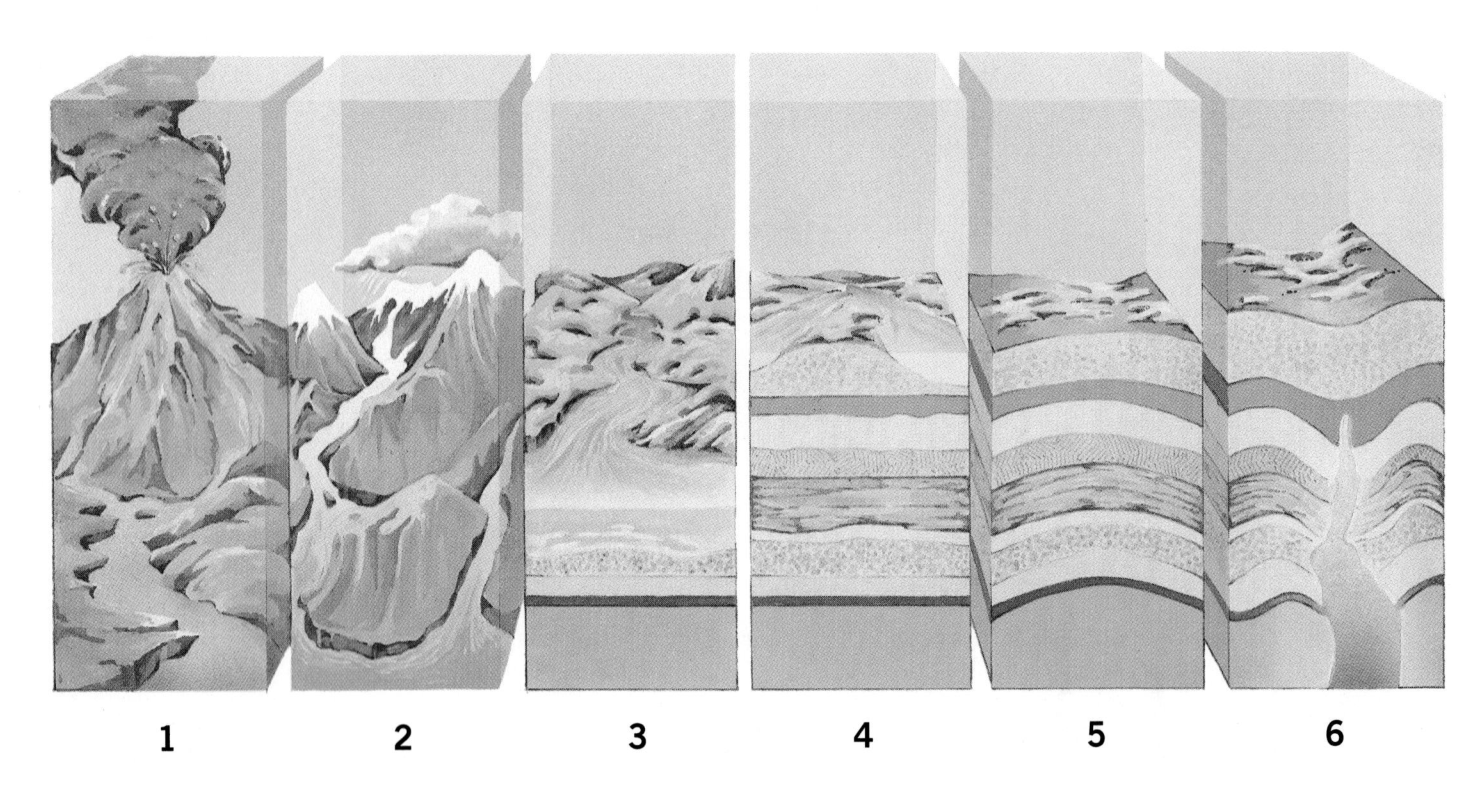

1. Lava forms igneous rocks.
2. Weathering and erosion break down and move rocks.
3. Rivers carry rocks to the sea or lake.
4. Deposition of particles occurs.
5. Compaction and cementation form sedimentary rock.
6. Heat and pressure change igneous and sedimentary rock into metamorphic rock.

Wildrose Canyon Kilns

In the 1800s, the Swiss, the Chinese, and American Indians worked together to produce charcoal. Charcoal is charred wood. When charcoal burns, it burns much hotter than wood. Because it burns so hot, miners used charcoal to melt ores.

In the Modoc Mines near Death Valley, charcoal was manufactured to melt silver and zinc ore.

Because there were no trees around the mines, a charcoal factory was built miles away in Wildrose Canyon, where there were pinyon (pin´yən) pines. Ten beehive-shaped ovens, called kilns, were built in 1877. Each kiln is about 10 meters across and 8 meters high. The kilns were designed by the Swiss and built of local rock by the Chinese.

The American Indians cut the pinyon trees. They stacked the kilns with wood and burned it until charcoal formed.

The kilns were abandoned in 1885. Then in 1971, the kilns were restored by Arizona Navajos.

How are you doing?

1. What is the rock cycle?
2. What are two changes that can occur in the rock cycle?
3. **Think** Igneous rocks are the oldest rock on the earth's surface. They are also the youngest. How can that be?

Looking Back

Words and Concepts

Complete the following statements.

1. The _______ shows changes that lead to one rock becoming another rock.
2. Under the right conditions, a rock can become any kind of _______.
3. _______ changes igneous rock into sediment.
4. _______ changes sedimentary rock into magma.
5. To become igneous rock, metamorphic rock must first melt and then _______.
6. Before becoming sedimentary rock, igneous rock must first weather and then _______.

Applied Thinking Skills

Answer the following questions. You can use words, drawings, and diagrams in your answers.

7. Explain how one sedimentary rock can be changed into another kind of sedimentary rock.
8. What change must occur for any kind of rock to become a metamorphic rock?
9. Does the rock cycle work both backward and forward? Explain your answer.
10. **Your World** What things in your life happen in a cycle?

Both wind and water can shape landscape features. These sandstone walls are the result of weathering mainly by water and by wind.

Show What You Know

Can you model the rock cycle?

Observe and Collect Data

1. Make five labels: *Igneous rock, Metamorphic rock, Sedimentary rock, Magma,* and *Sediment.*
2. Make five other labels: *Cooling; Melting; Burial, Heat, and Pressure* (one piece); *Compaction and Cementation* (one piece); and *Weathering.*
3. Arrange your labeled papers on the floor to show the rock cycle. Add arrows with tape.
4. Think of two paths that an igneous rock might take to become a different igneous rock. Stand on the paper marked "Igneous rock" and move through the cycle back to "Igneous rock."

Process Skills
Observing, Communicating, Making models

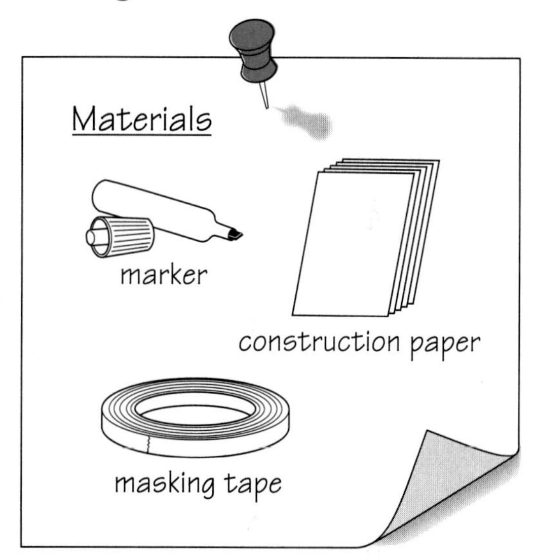

Draw Conclusions

1. Why is the rock cycle called a cycle?
2. Describe a cycle within the rock cycle that does not involve igneous rocks.

Rocks & Minerals

Show what you know about rocks and minerals. Work by yourself, with a partner, or in a group. Select one activity.

Historian Write a report comparing the uses of rocks and minerals in the past with the uses of rocks and minerals today. If needed, do extra research in the library. Read your report to the class.

Rockhound Write and act out a story that shows how the rocks in your area might have been created.

Game or Puzzle Inventor Create a game or puzzle that tells about the rocks and minerals of Death Valley. Play the game with your classmates and make changes before you make a final copy.

Songwriter Create a song that tells the story of the minerals of Death Valley. Make an audiotape or videotape and share it.

Landform Scientist Make a model using any materials you have, or create a drawing, of Death Valley. Show and label the rocks and minerals in the valley.

Writer Write a tale of rocks in Death Valley and how they change. Include weathering and the rock cycle.

Glossary

cementation (sē´men tā´shən) A process that causes sediments to stick together and form sedimentary rock. (page D34)

cleavage (klēv´ij) The way a mineral breaks along flat surfaces. It is a property that can be used to identify a mineral. (page D16)

compaction (kəm pak´shən) A process that presses sediments together. It is a step in the formation of sedimentary rock. (page D34)

crystal (kris´təl) The shape of minerals. (page D10)

density (den´sə tē) How heavy an object is compared to the space it takes up. It can be used to identify a mineral. (page D16)

fracture (frak´chər) The way a mineral breaks along curved or uneven surfaces. It can be used to identify a mineral. (page D17)

hardness (härd´nis) The ability of one mineral to scratch another. It can be used to identify a mineral. (page D16)

igneous rock (ig´nē əs räk) A rock that forms when melted rock cools and hardens. (page D30)

luster (lus´tər) The way a mineral reflects light. It can be used to identify a mineral. (page D15)

metamorphic rock (met´ə môr´fik räk) Rock that forms under pressure and heat within the earth. (page D38)

Mohs' scale (mōz skāl) A rating that indicates a mineral's hardness. (page D17)

rock cycle (räk sī´kəl) The process that causes one rock to become another. (page D54)

sedimentary rock (sed´ə men´tər ē räk) Rock that forms from sediments or pieces of older rock. (page D34)

sediment (sed´ə mənt) A tiny piece of rock that is worn away by wind or water. (page D34)

streak (strēk) The line left when a mineral is rubbed on a piece of unglazed tile. (page D15)

weathering (weth´ər ing) The wearing away of rock. (page D50)

Unit D Index

Boldface numerals denote glossary terms. Italic numerals denote illustrations.

Credits

Photographs

1 Dick Durrance II/The Stock Market; 2-3 David Muench; 2BL David Muench; 2TR David Muench; 3 National Park Service, Death Valley National Monument; 4BR David Muench; 4CL Joseph Sohm/Chromosohm/The Stock Market; 6BL National Park Service, Death Valley National Monument; 6BR Jim Randklev/AllStock; 7CR Larry Ulrich/DRK Photo; 7TL John Elk III; 10T Dr. Jeremy Burgess/SPL/Photo Researchers; 12 John Elk III; 20BL Robert Caputo/Stock, Boston; 20TL Larry Ulrich/DRK Photo; 21TR Isabella Stewart Gardner Museum, Boston/Art Resource; 26BL David Muench; 26TR Greg Probst/AllStock; 30B Michele Burgess/The Stock Market; 30T Tom Bean/DRK Photo; 31 Soames Summerhays/Photo Researchers; 32B Gregory G. Dimijian/Photo Researchers; 32C Peter Boonisar/AllStock; 32T David Ball/The Stock Market; 34-35 Larry Ulrich/DRK Photo; 36BCL Michael Ian Shopenn/AllStock; 36TL David Muench; 37C David Muench; 39 Tom Bean/AllStock; 40BL Jerry Jacka; 40CL Craig Bogan/Rainbow; 40TL Will Landon/AllStock; 41 David Muench; 42TR David Muench; 44 H. Simon/Tom Stack & Associates; 46BL Tom Bean/DRK Photo; 46C David Muench; 47BL John Elk III; 47CR James Randklev/AllStock; 50B Bill Horsman/Stock, Boston; 50C Tom Bean/DRK Photo; 50T James Randklev/AllStock; 52L David Muench; 52TR Don & Pat Valenti/DRK Photo; 53 Bob Burch/Bruce Coleman Inc.; 54B James Randklev/AllStock; 54C David L. Brown/The Stock Market; 54T David Muench; 57 John Gerlach/Tom Stack & Associates; 58 Tibor Bognar/The Stock Market

Anne Dowie* 36TR, 37T, 52BR
Geoffrey Nilsen Photography* 6TR, 11BC, 11TL, 11TR, 13B, 14, 15R, 15TC, 16R, 17L, 18BR, 18TC, 19(3 gems), 19(bauxite), 19BL, 21BR, 21TC, 21TL, 27BCL, 27BCR, 27BR, 33BR, 33CL, 36BL, 36BR, 37B, 40BCR, 40TCR
Ken Karp* 5, 9L, 9R, 10B, 13T, 15B, 18TR, 19TL, 20BR, 21BC, 24, 25, 29, 33TR, 40TR, 42TC, 45, 48,
Renee Lynn* 2BR, 2LC, 2TL, 4L, 4TR, 6(stamp), 6CL, 6TL, 7BR, 7TR, 11BL, 11BR, 11TC, 15TL, 16L, 17R, 18BC, 18BL, 18CL, 19(cans), 19(nails), 19(necklace), 19(turquoise), 19BR, 19BL, 19C, 20TC, 21BL, 26BR, 26TL, 27BL, 27CR, 27TL, 27TR, 33BL, 33TL, 36TCR, 40BR, 46BR, 46TL, 47(backgrd), 47BR, 47TL, 47TR

Special thanks to Jean DeMouthe from the California Academy of Sciences and to the National Park Service, Death Valley National Monument

Specimens for the following photographs were provided by the California Academy of Sciences: 6TR, 11BC, 11TL, 11TR, 13B, 14, 15R, 15TC, 16R, 17L, 18BR, 18TC, 19(gems), 19(bauxite), 21BR, 21TC, 21TL, 27BCL, 27BCR, 27BR, 33BR, 33CL, 36BL, 36BR, 37B, 40BCR, 40TCR

*Photographed expressly for Addison-Wesley Publishing Company, Inc.

Illustrations

Nea Bisek 8T, 25, 28, 43, 45, 48, 59
Len Ebert 22–23
Shelton Leong 60–61
Jane McCreary 8B, 29, 32, 49
Cyndie Wooley 3, 11, 13, 17, 31, 34–35, 38, 42, 51, 55, 56

Text

22–23 From Margy Burns Knight, *Talking Walls.* (Gardiner, ME: Tilbury House Publishers, 1992.) Copyright © 1992 by Margy Burns Knight.